Memory Lane
NANTWICH
compiled by Gordon Davies

Memory Lane
NANTWICH
compiled by Gordon Davies

First published in Great Britain in 2002 by
The Breedon Books Publishing Company Limited
Breedon House, 3 The Parker Centre, Derby, DE21 4SZ.

ISBN 1 85983 304 7

Printed and bound by Butler & Tanner, Frome, Somerset, England.

Jacket printing by Lawrence Allen.

Contents

Dedication

This book is dedicated to my wife Marjorie
(Madge)
for her daily support, patience and
encouragement,
not only for the time I have been working on my
three books
– *Memory Lane Crewe, Memory Lane Crewe
Volume Two* and *Memory Lane Nantwich* –
but for her love and understanding during our
49 years of marriage.

Introduction

The most picturesque parts of Nantwich have frequently featured in photographic books but *Memory Lane Nantwich* is spectacularly different. That is because it vividly documents the people of the town, the 'Dabbers' who make it one of the best-loved places in the country.

There are plenty of marvellous street scenes from yesteryear but Gordon Davies has also succeeded in producing a remarkable record of the townsfolk of Nantwich. These 216 pages are packed with hundreds of photographs that will bring back happy memories of days that are gone but not forgotten.

As a newspaperman I was reared on a couple of basic principles. One was that the best way to tell a story is through the people. That's why anyone who wants to know more about Nantwich in living memory will be fascinated by this book.

The other principle that holds true is that one picture is worth a thousand words. What Gordon has done through the camera lens could never have been equalled by even the most eloquent of prose.

Anyone who has enjoyed Gordon's earlier books, *Memory Lane Crewe* and *Memory Lane Crewe Volume Two* will be just as satisfied by this if they have any interest in near neighbour Nantwich.

Those who live in Nantwich and exiles from the town will, of course, find plenty of their own favourites. They may even spot themselves or a close relative or friend.

I was quickly enthralled as I turned the pages. There was the old Regal Cinema at the corner of Market Street where I went occasionally as a boy; there was Pillory Street where my mother lived as a girl in a tiny two-up, two-down terraced house; there was Carolyn Moore who was Miss Great Britain 1970s and the dream of every lad; there was Alan Ball senior leading Nantwich Town back in 1962.

All these bring back wonderful memories and, like all nostalgia, also a tinge of sadness for people and places we will not see again.

News stories covered by an illustrious predecessor of mine, the late Percy Walker, who was editor of the *Nantwich Chronicle* for many years, figure prominently in these pages. He was a great servant to the town and I believe he would have been delighted by this book. I can think of no finer recommendation than that.

Dave Fox
Editor
The Nantwich Chronicle
3A Mill Street
Nantwich CW5 5FT

Acknowledgements

In compiling this book I have enjoyed the help of many people who have offered photographs and information which has supplemented my own archives, and my thanks are extended to the following: *The Nantwich Chronicle* and my mate Alan Jervis who has been a mine of information, also Eric Nichols, Cecil Walker, Anne Bostock (my cousin from Bunbury), Michael Bebbington, David Sant, Mark Scholfield, Florence Mayman and not forgetting *The Nantwich Chronicle* editor Dave Fox who kindly supplied the introduction for this book.

Nantwich Places

High Street, Nantwich prior to the 1860s. The centre of the picture shows the old Buttermarket Hall which was demolished in 1868. The block of old houses and shops beyond were pulled down in 1872 and these days the area is the site of the Nantwich Square.

A lonely Nantwich Square showing the try-out of its new lighting in the early 1950s.

A view from the top of St Mary's Church in 1963 showing Nantwich Square in the foreground, the old Town Hall top right and the remains of the old Gas Works to the left.

Nantwich Square looking towards Pillory Street in 1976.

The former Quaker Chapel behind Pillory Street was built in 1724 with an adjoining cemetery when there were only 13 Quaker families in the area. It was the first non-conformist place of worship in the town. The last religious service was held there in 1922. After standing empty for many years, the building was converted and became the Nantwich Players Theatre in 1983.

In 1963 and 1965 there was a move afoot to put an end to the traffic snarl-up in the centre of Nantwich, as these pictures show, but it took another 20 years before pedestrianisation actually happened.

Work on the pedestrianisation of Nantwich Square in progress in 1983.

Pillory Street Methodist Church which was demolished in the 1960s.

Philip H. Chesters pictured with staff outside his grocery shop in 1910. His business was established in 1859 and stood at the corner of Hospital Street and Pillory Street. I don't think the health inspectors of today would take too kindly to the meat display outside the shop!

Bowers Row was one of the oldest rows of houses in Nantwich but was bulldozed some time after World War Two.

High Street, meeting with the junction of Oat Market (the road to to the right), and Swine Market (the road to the left), in 1908. In those days gas lamps attached to the buildings were used to illuminate the streets. The buildings in the centre of the picture were demolished many years ago.

Below: Part of Nantwich's twisting High Street in 1963 looking toward the River Weaver bridge. The buildings on the right of the photograph were demolished shortly afterwards Including the old Town Hall which can just be seen in the right centre of the picture.

The Crown Hotel, High Street, was once a coaching inn on the route from London to Chester and known as the Crown and Sceptre Inn. It was rebuilt after the great fire of Nantwich in 1583. Seen here in the 1960s the sign in the hotel entrance tells us that the restaurant was open for meals at 3s 3d (about 16p).

The Tollemarche Almshouses in Welsh Row are pictured here in 1964. Founded by Sir Roger Wilbraham in 1613, the almshouses were rebuilt by John Tollemarche of Dorfold Hall in 1870. The almshouses were modernised in 1986.

Welsh Row looking towards the town centre in the 1940s.

Looking towards the town centre in 1945 and Welsh Row was very quiet compared with the hustle and bustle of today's traffic. In times gone by Welsh Row was known as Frog Channel because of a perpetual stream which flowed down the street and into the River Weaver. The stream was redirected into a culvert in 1865.

Welsh Row Bridge spanning the River Weaver was built by a local stonemason, William Lightfoot in 1803. The first bridge, a wooden one, was erected in 1389 but was ruined by floodwater and replaced in 1623. That in turn was replaced by a stone and wood structure in 1663. In the background on the right is the old Town Hall building which was erected in 1868 having been paid for by public subscriptions. It housed a Corn Exchange, a Library, two committee rooms, the hall keeper's private residence and an Assembly Hall which could seat 1,000 people. The building was deemed to be unsafe and demolished in the 1960s in favour of a new road, Water Load. This photograph was taken in 1943.

Townwell House, Welsh Row, erected in 1740 in Regency Style, was built on the site of the town's original well.

Nantwich Cottage Hospital which stood in Welsh Row and was closed in 1971. The building was put up for auction in 1976 and bought by the P. Williams (Chemists) Company. The building has recently been demolished and is now a housing area.

Welsh Row looking towards the aqueduct in the 1940s, showing its fine Georgian and Tudor buildings.

A horse ferry. In February 1946 heavy rain caused the River Weaver to rise some 15 feet and in the space of a few hours the town became almost an island with practically every incoming road being submerged in at least three feet of water. The river became a raging torrent and so great was the rush of water against the Welsh Row bridge that there was danger of the structure collapsing. The fact that the gas and water mains crossed the bridge made the threat to its safety all the more serious. Hencotes and greenhouses were swept away and much livestock perished. Horse ferries were organised to carry people from their flooded homes.

The new floodgates in operation on the River Weaver in 1972.

The old Nantwich fire station, which was situated in Beam Street, in 1971. The station was demolished in the 1990s and has been replaced with housing for the Lady Vernon Trust – Lady Helen Walk. Here we see founder member and administrator, Councillor Alice Roberts, a former Crewe and Nantwich mayor, giving the signal to demolish the fire station. Nantwich now has a modern fire station on the opposite side of Beam Street.

This giant crater was formed at Church Minshull in 1958 when the canal burst its banks.

Reaseheath Agricultural College pictured during Christmas time in 1940, when the frozen lake became a skating rink for the students. Cheshire County Council purchased the Reaseheath Hall in 1919 and it opened as a School of Agriculture in 1921. During the war over 1,000 Land Army girls were trained at the college and replaced farmworkers who had been called up to fight in the war.

It was the final curtain for the Regal cinema with the showing of *The Riviera Touch* starring Morcambe and Wise, in September 1966. The cinema was Ye Olde Wyche Theatre which opened on the corner of Market Street in 1919. Before that date people enjoyed 'Magic Lantern' shows at the old town hall. The building re-opened as a bingo hall but more recently became the offices of Arthur Chatwin Ltd.

Harveys Tannery which stood in Millstone Lane and closed down in the 1970s.

The Sir Edmund Wright Almshouses in London Road which were pulled down and rebuilt in Beam Street. This photograph was taken in 1965.

The Sir Edmund Wright Almshouses in the early 1970s having been rebuilt on Beam Street with modern plastic downspouts are waiting for new windows to be fitted. The Almshouses now form part of a home for the elderly.

The Nantwich Brine Baths Hotel in Shrewbridge Road, Nantwich which had 54 bedrooms, large lawns and gardens, several glasshouses and a lake. It accommodated ladies of the Women's Auxiliary Air Force during World War Two and finally ended its days as a convalescent home. The hotel was demolished in the late 1950s to make way for a housing estate.

Sweetbriar Hall in Hospital Street as it was in about 1900. Built around 1450 the timber framing of the building had later been covered with pebble dash.

In 1958 the iron railings had been removed and the building is in a state of decay. The octagonal bay window was added in the 16th century. The building has since been restored.

A quiet misty morning in Hospital Street in the late 19th century. It looks as if the two young boys might be waiting to start their days work, note the sweeping brushes on the right of the picture, and someone has walked across the street during the time exposure on the camera creating a ghostly image in the centre of the photograph. Sweetbriar Hall can be seen, with its iron railings and octagonal bay window, further along on the right.

Churchyardside, and showing Pepper Street to the left, in 1860. Part of the graveyard has since been removed to allow for the widening of the road.

The demolition of some of the old houses in Pepper Street in 1964. The street was widened and the houses were replaced by modern shops.

An idyllic view of Peckforton Castle in the 1940s.

Peckforton Castle courtyard in the 1970s. In 1990 *Robin Hood*, starring Patrick Burgen was filmed here and the whole of the courtyard area was covered in ankle deep mud and straw to give it a more authentic look. The chapel on the left of the picture was disguised to look like an old barn.

The entrance to Peckforton Castle in the 1940s.

Churche's Mansion built in AD 1577 and seen here awaiting re-assessment in 1951. The building was a girls' school in the early 1900s but more recently has been a popular restaurant. The building is now an antiques centre.

After stripping the outer skin from the Churche's Mansion during restoration work at the rear of the building in 1955, workers found that the prefabrication idea is at least 400 years old.

This former Georgian mansion, pictured in 1966, later became Nantwich Liberal Club which unfortunately went out of business in the 1990s. It is now Peppers Restaurant.

Right: Pictured here in 1977 and built originally as a farm in the 15th century on land owned by Combermere Abbey, the Bowling Green Inn was licensed as an 'ale bar only' in 1775. The inn takes its name from the bowling green which used to be alongside.

Newly-occupied flats in Marsh Lane, Nantwich, in 1953 being some of the first permanent brick buildings to be erected in the town after World War Two.

Nantwich Grammar School pictured on the occasion of the school's 400th anniversary in 1960.

The Nantwich Mill was opened in 1789 by Thomas Bowyer and was originally a three-storey building, a fourth storey was added to the building in 1834. Spanning the River Weaver at the bottom end of Mill Street the cotton spinning mill engaged children from the Nantwich Workhouse on an apprentice scheme in the late 18th and early 19th century. After a strike by female workers the mill closed in 1874 but was later re-opened as a corn mill. The mill was destroyed by fire and demolished in 1970. The picture shows the mill in 1966 looking across the River Weaver.

A small section of the Barony Hospital, Nantwich in 1954, when, not only did the management committee deal with matters concerning the huge Barony Hospital, but also with those of the Crewe Memorial Hospital, Nantwich Cottage Hospital, Arclid Hospital (near Sandbach) and all of the local maternity homes. Unfortunately all of the local hospitals mentioned have now been demolished.

The Tollemache Arms at Faddiley, showing its splendid thatched roof in the 1960s. It has now been renamed The Thatch.

Love Lane, Nantwich in 1953 before the cobbles were tarmacked over and and it became part of a one-way system.

The junction of Beam Street and Manor Road in 1971 showing the Derek Copeland sectional buildings business. The area has now been replaced with shops.

The old Cosy Cinema in Mill Street, was originally The Ebineezer Chapel. It closed its doors to the public in April 1950. The building is now a nightclub.

St Joseph's School in London Road, pictured in 1987. It has now been taken over by a Bible society.

A scenic view of Beeston Castle in 1934.

Doddington Park Castle. The knights featured at the corners of the building were said to be esquires of the Black Prince, *c.*1934.

Church Minshull Village, 1945.

Harthill Church in the 1940s.

The quaint Crewe Arms Hotel, near Bunbury in 1943.

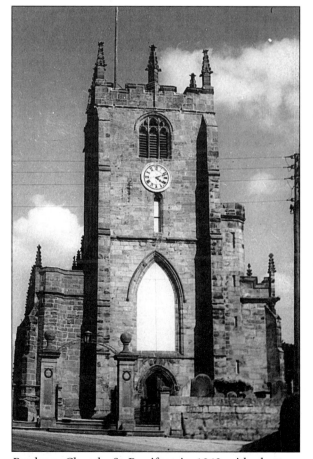

Bunbury Church, St Boniface in 1943 with shutters protecting the windows against bomb damage.

United Dairies Factory at Calveley in 1935. Now a housing estate.

This black and white timbered building, the Cheshire Cat, is seen here on 29 April 1962 and was originally known as the Widow's Almshouse. The building was converted from three 16th-century cottages in 1676 and six widows lived there. But in 1962 it was an eating house serving the best English food, morning coffee, lunches and dinners. A plaque on the right-hand side of the door tells us it was also the headquarters of the Nantwich Round Table. To the right of the photograph are some very worn stone steps which were mainly used by ladies for mounting and dismounting their horses having ridden side saddle into Nantwich, and, I suspect, customers who had spent too long at the bar! In 1972 Nantwich's most historic and picturesque pub opened as a disco club but later closed through lack of support. The building then stood empty for four years and along with the surrounding land became something of an eyesore. Now, brothers John, Paul and Mark Scholfield aim to develop the 450-year-old semi-derelict building into a top pub-restaurant and put a smile back on the face of the Cheshire Cat!

Over 100 years old, Boffey's Windmill is shown on the old one inch map as 53 North 62 Across between the A534 and the Swanley Hall, Stoney Green road. The windmill derived its name from the farmer who owned the land at the time. *c.*1940. The building has now been converted into a house.

Built of red sandstone in the 14th century, the beautiful St Mary's Church is often referred to as the Cathedral of South Cheshire. This picture, taken in 1943 from across the graveyard, shows the iron railings which used to surround the church.

The Black Lion public house viewed from the side of the Cheshire Cat in the 1940s.

The stone mounting steps of the Cheshire Cat.

The old Cheshire Cat van.

A peep behind the scenes. The Cheshire Cat kitchens in the 1940s.

An interior view of The Cheshire Cat in the 1950s.

One of the man traps which was on display along with bear traps and other antiques before the Cheshire Cat restaurant and tea house became a discotheque.

Nantwich's former police station up for sale in 1977. Note the siren on the top of the building which warned the people of Nantwich of an imminent air raid during World War Two. The police station stood in Welsh Row. It is now an antiques centre.

Part of the original Nantwich Workhouse which was built in 1780, and showing its old clock and bell tower. The building stood on the Barony. This has since been demolished.

The terraced houses in Pratchitts Row in 1960 looking rather forlorn. They have since been modernised. The three-storey building at the end of the row is the old Heighton's factory and has since become town houses.

Cedar Court, which escaped demolition, when the Barony Hospital was pulled down in the 1990s.

Chairman of the Urban Council, Mr Albert Peake, 'well and truly' lays the foundation stone of the Nantwich Civic Hall on 20 January 1950.

Painters putting the finishing touches to the Nantwich Civic Hall ready for the grand opening on 1 December 1951 by the then chairman of the Cheshire County Council, Sir Otho Glover. Some 700 people joined in the festivities and danced the evening away to the Harry Roy Orchestra.

Builders working on the extension of the Civic Hall in September 1964.

Audlem Fire Station pictured in 1954.

A quiet Audlem village in June 1968.

A quiet Main Road, Wybunbury, in 1962, and looking towards the famous leaning tower of St Chad's Church which was said to have been five feet out of true in 1840!

Nantwich People

Market Street School pupils around 1900.

Those were the days! The Nantwich Franklin Minstrels early in the 20th century.

The first motor bus service between Nantwich and Crewe began in 1905 and was owned by the Crewe Motor Bus Company. This packed open top vehicle is pictured before leaving the Nantwich Square for Crewe. It must have been quite a job holding on to those large hats!

A flower power group – see buttonhole blooms – before leaving Nantwich station in 1910.

Nantwich Urban Council fire brigade in the days of 'Bonnets and Bustles' parading through Nantwich in about 1910.

Nantwich town band pictured about 1911. Back row: A. Glover, T. Allcock, A.E. Adams, W. Heath, W. Sherrat, R. Blagg, C. Heath, H. Carefull, C. Sadler, W. Carefull (secretary), W.Ormes. Middle row: W. Butler, G. Harrison (bandmaster), W. Case. Front row: C. Heath (senior), W. Sadler, W. Allcock, W. Adams and F. Meachin.

Bunbury village band pictured outside the Bunbury Village Hall in 1912.

Ernest Bebbington (on the boat) enjoying a camping and fishing weekend on the River Weaver in the 1920s.

All aboard for a char-a-banc outing in the 1920s.

Miss Barbara Thomasson, who later became Mrs Foster, and was the first Nantwich Dairy Queen back in 1932.

A packed Nantwich Square for the visit of King George VI and Queen Elizabeth in the early 1940s.

Members of the Nantwich Parochial Church Council pose for a photograph in 1940.

A group of wartime workers at the Rowlinson's timber yard, Willaston, in 1943.

A night out for the girls from the Rowlinson's timber yard at Willaston in 1944.

Nantwich ARP (Air Raid Precaution) nurses and ambulance men pictured with their vehicle during World War Two.

A happy group pictured while on a day trip from the Nantwich branch of the Doody's Clothing Factory in the 1940s.

'Ned' Ireland, a stable attendant, pats racehorse Russian Hero after his great win in the 1949 Grand National. Looking on is head-stableman Bill Evans and trainer Mr George Owen's six-year-old daughter, Jane. Russian Hero trained at Cholmondeley and was given a civic reception when he returned to Nantwich.

Cholmondeley School headteacher, Mr Percy Wood, pictured with pupil Freda Thomasson on 19 June 1950.

Ladies from the Nantwich Doody's Clothing Factory pose for a photograph before returning to their machines in the 1950s.

A group of County Council members and officials, and first prize winners from the various sections, at a Reaseheath College Prize Day on 8 July 1950.

Mr A.E. Peake (chairman of the Nantwich Urban Council) with Red Cross officers and the Crewe team, who won the Worrall Cup on 4 November 1950. Second from the right is A/Comdt F. Crane of Nantwich (winner of the Myford Cup).

It was festival week in Nantwich in 1951 and the festival king and queen along with Councillor and Mrs Peake congratulated the winners of the various competitions at the local swimming baths. Young Paul Johnson was elected Master Nantwich 1951, Jacqueline Pamela Russell (centre) was winner of the Junior Miss Nantwich 1951, and Alison Jones (right) was runner-up.

Local people taking part in the Festival of Britain celebrations in 1951.

A group of Nantwich and Willaston Toc H members at a sports meeting at Crosslands, Stapeley, on 14 July 1951.

The Hon Mrs Angus Campbell (third from right), with a group of officers at a Scouts garden party on 25 August 1951.

A Nantwich carnival tableaux posing for the camera outside the Churche's Mansion before joining the procession in 1952.

The scene outside the Nantwich Civic Hall on 16 February 1952 when Queen Elizabeth II was proclaimed queen.

After the carnival it was time to relax with a well earned tipple *c.*1952.

Mrs P. Charlesworth, president of the Nantwich Club, pictured with visiting presidents at a Soroptimist Dinner at the Nantwich Civic Hall on 12 July 1952.

When Mr Jack Thomas purchased this bitch from a sale in the 1950s it immediately paid him back by winning a dog show in the name of Mischief Lass.

A Nantwich carnival float in 1953.

The Nantwich Young Farmers Club quiz team on 4 April 1953.

'You're never too old', said Mrs Georgina Hall as she decided to spruce up her home when she thought the estimate she received for some small paint jobs were far too excessive. Out came the ladder and paint brushes and, although in her 70s, she gave her home at 17 London Road, a face lift in time for the coronation of Queen Elizabeth II in 1953.

Mr Thorburn (left), receiving the Guiders' leather handbag from the president, the Hon Mrs Angus Campbell. Also pictured are the assistant county commissioner, Mrs J. Phillips, Miss E. Williams, divisional commissioner and Mrs Robert Young, the new district commissioner, 2 May 1953.

Cheesemaking at the Hall O'Coole Dairy on 12 June 1954.

A 1950s Nantwich carnival queen with her attendants.

Excited youngsters gather around the 1954 carnival queen.

It was 'Evening All' as the Crewe division of the Cheshire Constabulary bowls presentation evening gets under way on 18 September 1954.

The Cheshire Hunt waiting to enter the parade ring at the 1955 Nantwich Show.

Members of the Cheshire Hunt stole the show when they staged this 1850 pageant at the 1955 Nantwich Show.

Members of the Nantwich local Labour Party 'wait on' the ladies at a social and tea arranged in appreciation of the work of the women's section on 15 April 1955.

Nantwich firemen, past and present, at a brigade dinner on 7 May 1955.

Joan Lindop and Syd Jones leading the 1955 carnival parade across the Nantwich railway station crossing.

The traffic came to a standstill when these travelling Morris Dancers took over the centre of Nantwich on 10 September 1955. There would be no such trouble these days, the town centre is pedestrianised.

A Beeston Young Farmers Club quiz team on 1 April 1956, includes G.E. Wood, R. Garner, D.S. Rutter, J. Machin and Miss J.T. Humphries.

Checking a prize list at the Lifeboat Ball on 30 June 1956 are (left to right), Mr J. Kennedy, Mr M. Ackerman, Coxswain Parkinson, Mrs Ackerman and Major Disley.

Polish children at play during their stay at the Doddington Camp before being rehoused in the Crewe and Nantwich area in 1956.

Dance mistress, Miss Lindop prepares some of her pupils for the *Dance of the Pearls* on 18 August 1956.

At this local pantomime on 1 December 1956, the wicked uncle, George Woodcock, tells Aladdin (Wendy Bullock) and Widow Twankey (Renee Woodcock) how he will make them rich.

Mr J.K. Astbury (centre) with his four long-serving farmworkers on 8 June 1957. Left to right: Mr C. Shannon, Mr F. Pace, Mr T. Pace and Mr W. Bell.

Mrs Violet Parry prepares to give a train the 'go ahead' on the first day she became a railway signalwoman on 22 June 1957.

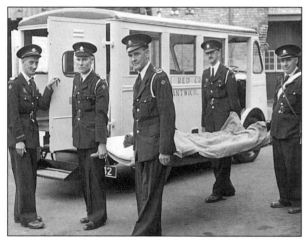

Nantwich Red Cross members with their ambulance during a training exercise on 22 June 1957.

Officer and trophy winners at the Nantwich and District Guide sports day on 29 June 1957.

Nantwich postmen who received their safe driving awards on 8 June 1957.

One of the big attractions at the 1957 Nantwich Festival was the milking of cattle on the Nantwich civic car park, particularly among the younger generation.

The new Cheshire Dairy Queen, Miss Jennifer Coppack, with her attendants Kathryn Woodward (left), and June Hayes, opened the 1957 Dairy Festival and are pictured here with Festival organisers.

Mr Fisher holding the trophy at the Acton Horticultural Show on 7 September 1957.

Willaston man Mr E.B. Lomax pictured with United States president Dwight Eisenhower on 23 November 1957.

The 1957 Nantwich UDC Chairman's Ball at the Nantwich Civic Hall. The chairman that year was Miss A.I. Astles (right of centre) seen here with her family group.

The Nantwich Veterans Aid Committee Ball at the Royal Hotel, Crewe on 22 February 1958.

Right: Carnival queen, Ann Wardell trying on her dress for the big day at the 1958 Nantwich carnival.

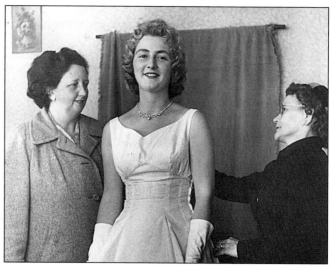

British Legion members at their annual dinner at Wrenbury on 8 March 1958.

The Nantwich Liberal Club Committee pictured on the 17 May 1958. The club folded in the late 1990s.

Mr Fred Lawton (centre) receiving his trophy at the 1958 Acton Horticultural Show.

Nantwich carnival queen, Ann Wardle receiving her crown in June 1958.

Right: Mr Mason showing his wife the blooms which won him the challenge cup and other trophies at the Nantwich Chrysanthemum Show on 20 September 1958.

The Way We Were – local girls modelling at a fashion show on 2 July 1958.

The BBC's editor and writers of *The Archers* pictured during a visit to a farm at Millmoor on 14 June 1958.

Nantwich Fire Brigade pictured at their old fire station in Beam Street in the 1950s.

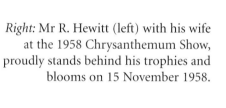

Right: Mr R. Hewitt (left) with his wife at the 1958 Chrysanthemum Show, proudly stands behind his trophies and blooms on 15 November 1958.

Carol singers outside Churche's Mansion in the 1950s.

Nantwich Rotary Club members and wives at their dinner at the Royal Hotel on 28 February 1959.

A group of prizewinners and officials at the Nantwich Young Farmers speech-making contest on 14 March 1959.

Lady Helen Broughton takes aim to try for a prize on one of the side-shows at the Conservative garden party at Hospital Street on 22 August 1959.

Exhibitors at this Wrenbury flower show on 22 August 1959.

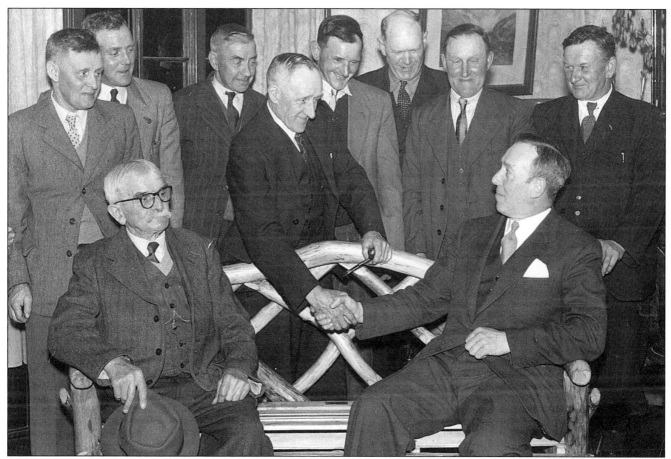

Acton Cow Club members look on as their president, Mr Blackburn, formally hands over a garden seat to honour the club's auditor on 2 May 1959.

Three hopeful entries for the Harvest Queen title on 12 September 1959.

District Girl Guides commissioner, Mrs Cox, pictured with youngsters at a Brownie Revels event on 6 June 1959.

Liberal Candidate, Guy Harvey, meeting farmworkers on 22 August 1959.

Cheers! as the Worleston WI raise their glasses to toast their 'Coming of Age' on 10 October 1959.

Mrs Alice Roberts (centre) pictured with members of her 'Brains Trust' panel at a group meeting of the Malbank WI on 31 October 1959.

Nantwich carnival committee chairman, Mr Joe Blagg (centre) with recipients of the carnival charity cheques on 14 November 1959.

A line-up of dignitaries at the 1959 Nantwich Civic Ball at the Civic Hall. Nantwich UDC chairman, Stan Dodd, is pictured centre.

Nantwich firemen honouring their officers on 7 November 1959. Mr A.R. Whittingham is pictured centre.

Finalists who competed in the Nantwich Harvest Queen competition on 15 August 1959.

Hatherton WI produce exhibition on 21 November 1959. The host, Mrs Furber is in the centre of the group.

The Audlem NFU meeting on 5 December 1959.

The North West Young Farmers Club Country Princess title was won by Susan Latham (second from right) on 27 February 1960. Also pictured (left to right) are: Miss Nora Blockley, Mr K. Nightingale, Mr D.R. Pimlott, Mrs M. McDonald, Miss Susan Latham and Miss June Hopley.

Setting up the Farmhouse Cheese stand at a 1960s Nantwich Show.

Mr P. Manning (seated centre) pictured at a Nantwich Young Farmers meeting on 16 January 1960.

Lady members at work in the produce tent at a 1960s Hatherton Show.

The British Friesian Club's 'Room at the Top' ball on 6 February 1960. Mr Tom Lee, the club's president, is third from the left.

The Reaseheath Association chairman's dinner dance on 20 February 1960.

The cast of *The Cage* presented by the Crewe West End Town's Women's Guild on 26 March 1960.

Girl Guide, Kathleen Williams
receiving her Queen's Guide award
on 3 March 1960.

Old soldiers at the Nantwich
British Legion dinner on
9 April 1960.

Nantwich firemen pose for a picture before sitting down to the brigade dinner on 16 April 1960.

Contestants for the Nantwich carnival queen competition on 7 May 1960.

Trophy winners at a Red Cross rally on 23 July 1960.

Local optician, David Owen, literally made his own 17th-century music when he crafted this beautiful harpsichord in 1960.

Nantwich Red Cross cadets and officers on 23 July 1960.

A Nantwich Red Cross Proficiency awards evening on 30 April 1960.

Happy pupils outside the new Nantwich Girls School in Audlem Road on 10 September 1960. It is now Brine Leas High School.

The platform party at the Nantwich Young Farmers AGM on 10 December 1960.

Officials at the North Western Farmers Sports Club dinner on 22 April 1961.

S. Jackson and Sons were proving that steam still had a part to play in farming when they displayed these two modern steam tractors on 28 January 1961.

Officials and winners at the Nantwich Young Farmers Speech Making Competition on 25 March 1961.

Girl Guide Divisional Commissioner, Miss E. Williams, presenting Hilary Wilding with her trophy watched by, left, Gill Sinclair and Margaret Holland on 15 July 1961.

Professor Bywater handing out the prizes at the Cheshire School of Agriculture on 1 July 1961.

A presentation at the Nantwich Fire Station on 22 July 1961.

Mrs R.W. Evans presenting the trophies to winner Mr T. Oakes at the Acton Horticultural Show on 2 September 1961.

Wrenbury Councillors adding yet another award to their Best Kept Village sign on 11 November 1961. Pictured are (left to right): C.W. Jones (chairman), C. Chesters (clerk), Mr Roff, R. Griffiths and G.D. Lucas (vice-chairman).

The platform party at a Red Cross evening on 2 October 1961. Nantwich Urban Council chairman and his wife, Mr and Mrs George King were guests.

Police constable Fernihough is at the scene as these two vehicles negotiate a tight squeeze in Nantwich High Street in October 1961. The area is now pedestrianised.

Nantwich Premier Flying Club couple with their awards on 16 December 1961.

Nantwich Ranger Guides show off their new standard which was made by Janet Buckley, second left. Also pictured are left to right: Jean Boffey, Gillian Ellson and Brenda Bailey. This picture was taken on 9 June 1962.

Can-Can dancers who took part in the local production of *Bitter Sweet* in 1961.

Mrs E. Betts is all smiles as she receives her sash after winning the Glamorous Grandmother competition at the Goodwill Faddiley Hall on 16 December 1961.

St Mary's Church organist for 40 years, Mr H. Tew is seen here on the occasion of his retirement in 1962.

A triumphant cadet team as they pose with the British Red Cross Challenge Shield on 29 September 1962.

Club officials viewing some of the outstanding blooms at the Nantwich Chrysanthemum Society's show on 22 September 1962.

This Nantwich Young Farmers team reached the final in the 1962 Debating Competition.

Carnival committee members enjoying a social evening after a successful Nantwich carnival in 1962.

Winners and officials at the Acton Horticultural Show on 8 September 1962.

Nantwich Young Farmers Club members waiting to compete at their sports day event at the Reaseheath College in 1963.

Mr and Mrs Edgar Edge with their sons, daughters, grandchildren and great-grandchildren when they celebrated their golden wedding in 1962. Mr and Mrs Edge lived at Ravensmoor.

Members of the Acton Amateur Operatic Society pose for a photograph for the press before getting down to rehearsals for their next production in the 1960s.

This troupe of girls are waiting for the 'quick march' signal in Welsh Row during the 1963 Nantwich carnival.

The top table at a Rotary Club dinner at the Cheshire Cat Eating House, on 23 February 1963.

Geoffrey Highfield receiving his Assistant Scoutmaster's Warrant on 5 October 1963.

A pre-dinner chat for these officials at the Friesian Club Dinner Dance on 2 February 1963.

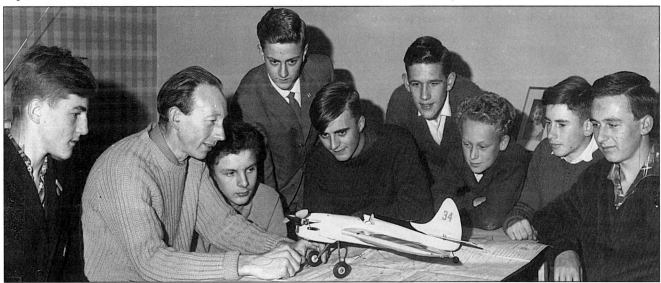

Young aero-modellers pictured with instructor Mr Hollowood on the very first meeting of the Nantwich Aero-Modellers Club on the 14 September 1963.

In 1963 The Nantwich Operatic Society staged the show *Oklahoma* and here we see the show's dancing mistress, Cynthia Hancock, passing on a few tips to her dancers.

Cecil Walker as the Persian pedlar backed by the male chorus during a scene from *Oklahoma* staged by the Acton Operatic Society in 1963.

Young entertainers in 1964, left to right, Brendan White, Pamela Ellis, Harold Harris and Gillian Shapcott.

Final night scenes at the show *Oklahoma* staged by the Acton Operatic Society in 1963. Top picture: The finale. Bottom left: Trevor Jones, who went on to become a professional actor, receiving a gift at the end of the show. Bottom right: Back stage celebrations.

Mr Thomas Robert Owen, standing and Mr John James Owen pictured in 1964 when between them they had completed 100 years service with British Railways.

Nantwich Players pictured rehearsing on 24 April 1964.

Machinists on the main machine line at the factory of Heaps of Nantwich Ltd in 1964. The factory closed some years ago.

A Nantwich Parish Church garden party on 4 July 1964.

Peter Usher (Chopin) and Marjorie Geoghegan (Countess Wanda) in *Waltz Without End*, an Acton Operatic production on 6 November 1964.

Youngsters who took part in the dancing at the Scottish Society Ceilidh dancing in 1964.

Emergency services working frantically to free trapped passengers from a car after it had been hit by a train at the Nantwich railway station in July 1964. George Eardley, from Crewe, who was awarded the Victoria Cross for bravery in World War Two, lost a leg in the incident.

Nantwich Army Cadets taking part in an off duty games evening on 28 November 1964.

A presentation of gavels to these past chairmen of the Nantwich branch of the National Farmers Union on 12 December 1964.

Officials and guests at the Nantwich Chamber of Trade dinner dance on 4 November 1965.

A costume group outside the Cheshire Cat Eating House on a Holly Holy day.

Revellers at the Hunt Ball at Doddington Hall on 16 January 1965.

The youngest guest at the Nantwich Motor Club Ball on 14 October 1965, was seven-year-old Pauline Hoffman, pictured here receiving a prize. The bottom photograph shows popular bandleader of those days, Victor Silvestor, with his orchestra.

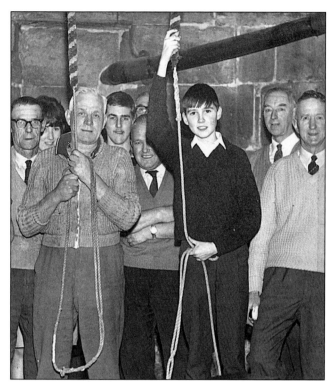

Red Cross officers with their winning team of cadets outside the Nantwich Civic Hall on 4 August 1966.

Grandfather Mr Frank Ollier pictured with bellringers at the Nantwich St Mary's Church on 6 January 1966.

George Tomlinson receiving his trophy after winning the British Red Cross Society show on 27 August 1966.

Members of the Acton Operatic Society on stage on 28 October 1966.

Members of the cast line up for a photograph at the Acton Operatic Society rehearsals in 1966.

Well known local rider, Wilf White, who lived at Burland, and his horse Nizfella, putting in a guest appearance at the Nantwich Show after winning an Olympic gold medal in the 1960s.

Mr Richard Barnett receiving a trophy at the 1967 Nantwich Show.

Nantwich Urban District Council chairman, Tom Holman, made the presentations when these five Nantwich Scouts gained Queen's Scout Awards on 16 March 1967.

Mr Evans, (second left), receives his presentation for half a century's service with the NUAW on 19 October 1967.

Young Farmers waiting to entertain in the Nantwich Show ring on 20 June 1968.

Halloween came early for this lorry load of witches in the Nantwich carnival of June 1968.

Nantwich Council horse Toby pictured with his handler Mr Walsh on the day he went into retirement on 16 May 1968.

Councillors Alan Chapman, George King and Joe Blagg lead a march through the town square in 1968 to protest against the proposed pedestrianisation of the town centre.

Jean Harris, Miss Nantwich of 1969, listed one of her hobbies as horse riding.

A triumphant Yvonne Ormes was greeted by the Nantwich UDC chairman and his wife, Mr and Mrs George King, when she returned home after winning the Miss United Kingdom title in 1970. Yvonne has a string of beauty titles to her name. In 1966 she won the local Miss Nantwich title followed by the Miss England title in May 1970, then it was on to the Miss United Kingdom title in August 1970, also in 1970 she came sixth in the Miss World competition in America, and went on to win the Miss Nightclub of Great Britain title in 1971. She was much sought after for personal appearances and modelling work.

Miss Nantwich 1970, Diane Chadwick, handing out cheques at a presentation evening.

Young Jean Beech presents the Nantwich UDC chairman's wife, Mrs George King, with a bouquet at an Elm House garden party in 1970.

The Cheshire Regiment on parade along Beam Street in the 1970s.

A group of lady members of the Acton Amateur Operatic Society outside the St Mary's Church in the 1970s.

Its a fun day in Nantwich as people line the streets to watch the 1970 carnival pass by. The Nantwich carnival was discontinued some years ago.

Cholmondeley School headmaster, Percy Wood, joining in the fun at the school Christmas party in 1970.

Mr and Mrs Bill Thomas pictured on the occasion of their retirement as steward and stewardess from the Nantwich Liberal Club in December 1970.

Nantwich beauty, Carolyn Moore, who won the Miss Great Britain title in the 1970s.

Round-the-world yachtswoman, Nicolette Milnes Walker, receiving a toast from Nantwich Rural Chairman, Walter Hulme, when she was guest of honour at the Rural Council Offices on 16 September 1971. Also pictured are councillors and guests.

The 1972 Miss Nantwich with her attendants after the crowning ceremony at the Nantwich Civic Hall.

Captain Hollinshead and his son Francis with their traction engine on 30 August 1973.

Local people, including the local 'Bobby', were fascinated by this pair of swans which were looking for a nesting site and had taken up residence on the local village pond at Hankelow in 1973.

Staff at work in the Heaps Clothing Factory in May 1973. The factory closed some years ago.

Jacqueline Horwich with her prize-winning horse, Kararoc Witchazel in 1974.

Machinists and management at the Kindler clothing factory in 1974.

Councillors and their guests at the last social evening of the old Urban District Council before the Crewe and Nantwich Council was formed in 1974.

Nantwich Show official pictured after a meeting to prepare for the 1974 event.

A group of Red Cross award winners in 1974.

The deputy mayor and mayoress of Crewe and Nantwich, Councillor and Mrs Albert Platt, pictured with governors and guests at the Goudhurst College centenary celebrations in June 1975.

Brookfield House in Shrewbridge Road, which was the home of the Nantwich Urban Council until 1974 when the councils of Crewe and Nantwich amalgamated to become the Borough of Crewe and Nantwich.

Employees hard at work at the new Porta Showers' Nantwich factory when it opened in 1976.

The last-ever meeting of the Nantwich Education Executive Committee in March 1976. Education officer, Ronald Astley is left of centre.

Nantwich outdoor brine baths in full swing in 1976.

The old C of E Market Street School, which is now a fine art saleroom. In the severe winter of 1878 to 1879 a group of local ladies opened a soup kitchen at the school, and provided hot meals for the Nantwich poor until the following spring. Photograph taken in 1977.

A line up at the last-ever Founder's Day in 1977 before Nantwich Grammar School became the Malbank School. Pictured on the left is headmaster, Mr Herbert Rowsell. Also pictured are the Bishop of Chester and the former rector of Nantwich St Mary's Church, the Revd Tim Richardson.

Mr Albert Jolly with some of his many friends after a concert recital in 1978.

Policeman Derek Taylor and his wife Margaret pictured outside their Alpraham home before he retired in 1978. They now live in Nantwich.

Vauxhall Road residents at their street party to celebrate the Prince of Wales' wedding in 1981.

Cronkinson's Oak residents celebrate the marriage of the Prince and Princess of Wales with a street party in 1981.

Former Brookfields council offices caretaker, Mr Harold Taylor, pictured with his wife Evelyn, on the occasion of his retirement on 5 February 1981.

Princess Margaret visiting a local Guides camp in the 1980s.

Waiting for Princess Margaret to arrive at the Girl Guides summer camp, 1980s.

Nantwich Players pictured after a rehearsal at their new premises The Quaker House in Pillory Street – now the Players Theatre in 1981. The play *Voyage Round My Father* by John Mortimer was directed by Ray Cowdall and staged at the Civic Hall because the Players Theatre wasn't quite ready after its conversion. Ray Cowdall is pictured at the on the right-hand side of the back row.

Nantwich Town Council chairman, Alan Chapman joining in the fun at a street party to celebrate the Prince of Wales' wedding in 1981.

Local businessman, Geoff Farr, beat the traffic jams in 1981 when he used to take off from a field near his home.

A giant greetings card for the Prince and Princess of Wales was on display on the Nantwich Square during July 1981. The Nantwich Town Council chairman, Alan Chapman, looks on as his wife, Phyllis, shows the card to shoppers.

Nantwich Town Council chairman, Alan Chapman, pictured with councillors outside the Council offices after the last meeting of the Nantwich Council in Brookfield House in May 1982.

Various local church members who combined at the Nantwich St Mary's Church to record a programme for the BBC's *Songs of Praise* in 1982.

Go-kart champion, Mark Appleton, with his trophies and his kart in 1982.

David Hilman from Poole (left) receives the National Pig Award from the Duke of Gloucester on 1 April 1982.

Actress Wendy Craig, presenting the Cheese Awards at a 1980s Nantwich Show.

Brine Leas School 'Crime Squad' with their solution to cracking crime in the 1980s.

Brian Johnston pictured with local business people when BBC's *Down Your Way* visited Nantwich in 1982. It just happened to be on Brian's birthday!

My friend, local businessman, canal boat builder, Sidney Cummins – with his grandson, also Sidney, taking the 'dog' a walk at the Nantwich Basin End.

The 1983 Cheshire dairy queen, Debbie Hulme.

St Mary's Church bellringer, Frank Ollier, pictured outside the church on 20 October 1983.

Joanne Tilley showing off her Queen's Guide award in July 1983.

Youngsters having a splashing time at the Nantwich Open Air Brine Pool in the hot summer of 1983.

Housing Minister, Ian Gow, opens Bowling Green Court on 12 June 1984, looking on is the mayor of Crewe and Nantwich, Anne Blacklay, councillors and invited guests.

Amanda Bettaney with her horse at Faddiley on 6 August 1984.

The mayor and mayoress of Crewe and Nantwich, Mr and Mrs Les Wood, leaving the Nantwich St Mary's Church in 1986.

Mrs Joan Heath with her colleagues at WH Smith Ltd on 16 January 1986.

A diamond turn out for the Nantwich Young Farmers' diamond jubilee celebrations at the Nantwich Civic Hall in 1985.

Well-known local artist, the late Haydn Jones, pictured with one of his much sought-after pen and ink drawings of Nantwich in 1986.

Michelle Harding after winning the Working Hunter Championship Trophy in 1986.

In August 1987 Kathy Weston had her engagement ruined by a jealous parrot! Lovesick macaw, Jaffa wasn't too pleased when his favourite bird Kathy announced she was getting married to her boyfriend Paul Harrison. The eight-month-old blue and gold South American parrot went on the attack and with one bite of his powerful beak bit her engagement ring in half, swallowing the valuable topaz diamond centre. Horticultural worker Kathy worked at the £1 million The Palms tropical house at the Stapeley Water Gardens, and Jaffa, who was the first bird bought for the tourist attraction, had always been wild and had shunned human contact. But, when Kathy started work it was love at first sight. He took to her straight away and his favourite perching place was on her shoulder. Laughed Kathy: 'Paul was as sick as a parrot when I told him about it, but now he has forgiven Jaffa.' Kathy's boss, Ray Davies, offered to pay for a new ring.

Reaseheath Agricultural College principal, the late George England (fourth from right) and his wife Edith, pictured with colleagues at his retirement presentation on 5 March 1987.

Forget the computer games etc., Punch and Judy can still hold its own as this picture proves, when this crowd was entertained on the Nantwich Square on 21 June 1987.

Members of the Cheshire Regiment Association pictured at a social evening at the Alvaston Hall Hotel on 15 September 1987.

WRVS members with their medals on 27 January 1988.

Mr Ray Elston exhibiting his paintings on 15 June 1988.

The Battle of Nantwich scenes from earlier years.

Each year Cavaliers and Roundheads fight a mock battle in the centre of Nantwich to commemorate the town's civil war battle over 350 years ago. Members of the Sealed Knot pour into town from all parts of the country with their cannon, muskets, pikes and swords to re-enact the battle, which is staged on Mill Island. In January 1644 the town was the scene of a bloody battle as a Parliamentary army lead by Sir Thomas Fairfax freed the people of Nantwich who had been virtual prisoners of the Royalists for several weeks. The lifting of the scene was marked by townspeople wearing a sprig of holly in their caps and since the re-enactment was rekindled in 1970s (staged on Barony Park in those days) – the day has been known as Holly Holy Day. In the year 2000 some 500 troops took part and the mock battle was watched by several thousand people.

Ronnie and Jayne Leek with their dog Millie and her 11 pups.

The Sealed Knot's Major Gillitt talking to Christine MacGonigle on the Nantwich Square before the 1988 mock Battle of Nantwich.

Malbank School headmaster, Mr Herbert Rowsell pictured with some of his pupils on 27 January 1988.

Mums and Tots Swimming Club at the Nantwich Baths in the early 1990s.

Rotary Club members pictured with their guest, the mayor of Crewe and Nantwich, Alan Pheasey, at a Rotary evening in 1990.

Popular Nantwich artist Sheila Trigg working on a portrait painting watched by her pet cat Cindy.

Schooldays

Nantwich Grammar School football team, 1941-42.

Penny Taylor, who won the Crewe and District Schools Association title for the best performance in athletic inter-county matches. She is seen here with the All-England Hendon Cup in 1964.

Nantwich and Acton Grammar School and staff in 1956.

Cheshire Grammar Schools cricket team of 1959.

Nantwich Grammar School girls hockey team with their trophy in the 1960s.

Manor Road School Intermediate School football team 1963-64.

Nantwich and Acton Grammar School team which won the Cheshire hockey tournament in November 1965.

Another Nantwich Grammar School's girls hockey team in 1966.

Nantwich Football Club

NANTWICH Football Club was founded in 1884 and it wasn't until 1973 that the word 'Town' was added to the title. Nantwich FC played its very first match on Saturday, 18 October 1884. The match was reported in the *Crewe Chronicle* and the side representing Nantwich was: F. Sadler, J. Bettley, J. Noden (captain), H. Billington, T. Williams, B. Wright, J. Williamson, C. Chesworth, W. Bullock, H. Downing and W. Davies. The report added that Nantwich won by 'one goal and four disputed to nil'!

Over the years Nantwich FC has been comprised mainly of players living locally or perhaps a bus ride away from the ground – places like Crewe, Sandbach and Middlewich. Some players have gone on to play for League clubs, having started with Nantwich, while others have ended their careers at the club having played professional football for many years.

The club was better known as the Wychers because of the town's salt which was believed to alleviate fits, indigestion and rheumatism. Later they were known as the Cobblers, referring to the town's shoe-making trade which ceased in 1925. Since that time they have been known as the Dabbers, a Nantwich expression for depositing a bet with a stakeholder.

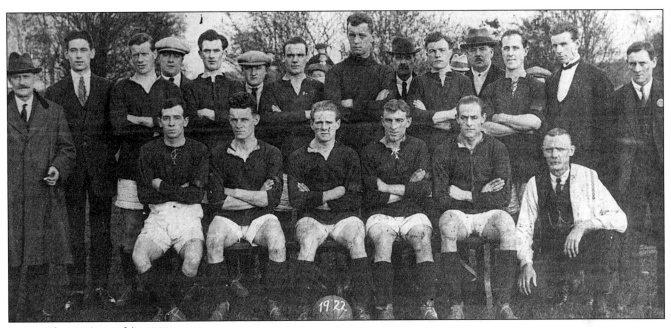

Nantwich FC pictured in 1922.

Nantwich FC, Cheshire Senior Cup winners in 1933 when they beat Whitchurch in the Final.

Nantwich FC, 1950. Back row (left to right): John Heath, Herbie Sandlands, Westwell, Bill Mason, Sid Farrington, Les Mills. Front row: Geoff Heath, Jack Young, Arthur Lucas, Dennis Nicholls and Bob Bowyer.

'Keep your eye on the ball' advises Jimmy Cooke, Nantwich FC's new player-coach in the early 1950s. Pictured are: Phil Latham, John Boardman, Bob Bowyer, Arthur Lucas, Jack Foxley, Dennis Nicholls, Jimmy Cooke (holding the ball), Harry Latham, Jack Young and Billy Gray (secretary).

Nantwich FC in 1951 when Ernie Tagg was skipper. He went on to manage Crewe Alexandra twice in later years.

Nantwich FC, 1951. Standing (left to right): Mr A. Hinde (president), S. Farrington, J. Heath, A. Lucas, H. Jones, E. Tagg, C. Fox, L. Mills, T. Nicholls (trainer), Mr J. Hunt (trainer). Seated: A. Brereton, D. Bowen, J. Cooke (captain), C. Green and G. White.

Nantwich FC, 8 May 1954.

Nantwich FC, 1955. Back row (left to right): W. Gray (secretary), Beswick, Dean, Pike, R. Ashcroft, L. Ashcroft and Cornes. Front row: Blunstone, Davies, Dutton, Heath, Mason and Young.

Nantwich FC, pictured in 1957.

Backroom staff repairing the nets and giving the dressing rooms a lick of paint in preparation for the 1958-59 season at Nantwich FC.

Nantwich FC's reserve team in 1958.

Nantwich FC, pictured in 1958.

Nantwich FC, pictured in 1959.

Nantwich FC squad photographed on 27 August 1960.

Nantwich FC team, 15 October 1960.

Nantwich UDC chairman, Mr Joe Blagg, declares the new Nantwich FC dressing rooms open on 19 November 1960.

Nantwich FC,
14 October 1961.

Hartford goalkeeper Johnson
goes down at the feet of
Nantwich right-winger Price in
this 1962 match at Jackson
Avenue.

Popular local player Billy Haddock had a near miss with this effort against Middlewich on 7 April 1962. Note the old stand in the background.

A celebrating Nantwich
FC on 12 May 1962.

Nantwich FC manager, Alan Ball (senior), talking to the players as trainer and ex-player Geoff Heath gives treatment to Arthur Payne on 8 December 1962.

Tony Adams, the Nantwich goalkeeper, managed to push this effort round the post when Chester Reserves visited London Road ground on 16 March 1963.

The Nantwich FC team which beat Barnton 4-1 at the London Road ground on 21 September 1963.

Nantwich FC youth team, 15 February 1964.

The successful Nantwich FC team which played Witton on 22 August 1964.

The Nantwich FC team which lost in the first round of the Cheshire Senior Cup when they went down 4-2 to Ellesmere Port in 1965.

A break from training for this Nantwich FC team during their first session of the 1965 season.

The Nantwich FC youth team which beat Alsager in 1966.

The 1967 Nantwich FC team.

A 1970 Nantwich FC team.

Nantwich Town team, August 1974.

The players pose for a photograph at the Nantwich Town ground in May 1976.

A 1970s Nantwich Town team.

Nantwich Town FC team, 1977.

Nantwich Town FC players at a 1977 training session, including Ben Wilson, Micky Webb, Peter Waddington, Kevin Westwood and Paul Mayman. Two names are not known.

Glyn Morris, who was the Nantwich Town FC manager in 1986.

A Nantwich Town FC team from September 1986.

Nantwich Town FC team in the late 1980s.

A 1980s Nantwich Town FC team.

A 1990 Nantwich FC team.

Local Football

A Barony Park Rangers football team of the 1920s.

Wrenbury FC, winners of the Crossley Cup in the late 1940s. Mr C.W. Jones is pictured presenting the Crossley Cup to the Wrenbury team captain, H. Taoley. Also in the picture, on the extreme left, is Johnny King, who went on the play for Crewe Alexandra and Stoke City.

Stoke City star Freddie Steele signing autographs during a visit to Nantwich in the 1950s.

Willaston White Star FC, 25 September 1954.

Nantwich Veterans FC pictured on 21 April 1956. Standing (left to right): H. Sandlands, J. Cowap, S. Farrington, H. Jones, H. Williams, W. Gray. Front row: G. Heath, J. Davies, J. Young, D. Nicholls and J. Middleton.

Nantwich Old Grammarians football team, 29 November 1958.

Sound Rovers, 13 May 1961.

Nantwich Corinthians FC, 18 May 1963.

Sound Rovers, 9 May 1964.

Murgatroyds FC, Sunday League Challenge Cup winners in May 1964.

Audlem Rangers cup-winning team of 1966.

Doddington Park football team with their trophy on 18 May 1967.

The Unions football team, which mainly consisted of former Boys' Club members, 9 November 1967.

This Barclays Bank football team played in the Crewe and District Regional League, Division Three, in 1977. Back row (left to right): Dave Smith, Brian Waring, Nigel Brookshaw, John Tatler, Steve Churchill, Phil Jackson, Peter Wood (player-manager). Front row: Tony Hopkins, Bob Brookshaw, Ray Gregory, Roy Evanson and Paul Jackson.

Bowls

Park Road Bowling Club members with their trophies outside the old pavilion in 1949. They opened their new pavilion in 2001.

Tommy Hayes, a popular local bowler who did his fair share of winning.

Jack Cookson, Len Smith, Tom Hayes and Frank Merrill with their trophies after competing in a Nantwich bowls tournament on 2 September 1961.

Club officials and bowls section prize winners at the Willaston Working Men's Club presentation evening on 18 October 1961.

Angling

Messrs Barker, Neville, Latham, W. Smith and T.W. Smith at a fishing match prize presentation evening on 27 September 1952.

Prizewinners at a Gas Board fishing match at Nantwich on 19 September 1953.

The Boot and Shoe Anglers with their fishing match prizes in 1954.

The Boot and Shoe public house fishing match prize distribution on 24 September 1955.

Harry Butler donned his best suit before posing with his 11½lb pike on 5 November 1955.

Mrs Ethel Wright with her trout catch on 25 May 1957.

White Horse Inn anglers with their fishing match prizes on 11 August 1956.

Prize winners at the White Horse public house fishing match presentations on 27 July 1957.

A group of prize winners at the Willaston Working Mens' Club annual fishing match social evening on 3 August 1957.

Mr Bill Jones presenting prizes after a junior fishing match on 24 August 1957.

Angler, Bill Bates, taking part in a canal match on 5 September 1957.

Nantwich Angling Society trophy presentations on 21 December 1957.

Fishing match prize time at the White Horse public house in Pillory Street on 19 July 1958.

Young Harold Clarke after a fishing match on 30 August 1958.

President Bill Jones presenting the Wyche anglers trophies for their annual club match on 6 September 1958.

Anglers with their prizes after the 1958 annual general meeting and prize presentations at the Wyche Anglers Club.

The Nantwich British Legion angling awards on 20 September 1958.

George Simpson receiving his trophy from licensee Bill Jones after a fishing match from the Three Pigeons public house on 11 October 1958. Other prizewinners are looking on.

A group of trophy winners at the Nantwich Post Office angling awards night in the 1950s.

With officials and other prizewinners looking on, the president, Mr Bill Jones, presents the Mere trophy to Mr Frank Crane for weighing in the years biggest pike in 1958. Also pictured, extreme left, is Mr Jack Whitney who donated the new Bream Cup at the Wyche Anglers AGM.

The presentation of the Nantwich British Legion Angling Cup on 19 September 1959.

Maurice Ralphs with his giant 20ins trout on 18 June 1960.

Young anglers with their trophies after their success in the Cheshire Anglers Juvenile match at Nantwich on 29 August 1959.

Mr H. Sharratt proudly shows off his angling prizes on 9 July 1960.

Nantwich Chronicle journalist, the late Percy Walker, holding up two dead bream, the result of water contamination of the Nantwich Canal in the 1960s. The white shapes in the water were some of the other dead fish. It was an anglers' nightmare at the time.

Vic Jones proudly shows of his monster pike in the 1960s.

Right: Mrs Eva Nowell hauling in a very small fish (they all count) during a canal match organised by the Baronia Factory on 27 August 1960.

How's That! Mr H. Hodgkinson prepares to liberate his catch after winning this match on 27 August 1960.

Two smiling youngsters who made the Cheshire Anglers Juvenile match prize list in the 1960s were Arthur Cope (left) and David Bate.

Proudly holding their plaques are these Wyche Anglers Club team members in 1961, who had recently won, for the third time in four years, the Cheshire Anglers Association Premier Team Trophy.

Presentations at the Wyche Anglers Club junior fishing match on 2 September 1961.

George Osbourne reels in a nice perch during this Wyche Anglers Club match on the Shropshire Union Canal match on 11 November 1961.

Young David Williamson collecting his trophy from Guy Harvey at the Nantwich Angling Society presentation on 20 December 1961.

Local businessman, Walter Elson, presenting the prizes at a Three Pigeons public house angling meeting on 1 July 1961.

Dennis Robinson with his 6lb bream weigh-in on 15 July 1961.

Alderman J.T. Jackson presenting young angler, David Holman, with one of his many awards won during the 1961 season.

Stefan Betteley (12 years) and Leon Betteley (17 years) collect their angling prizes in June 1962.

Wyche anglers, Syd Steele and David Holman, with their cased souvenirs on 27 October 1962.

Mr and Mrs Moss casting an expert eye over some new fishing rods on 3 November 1962.

Harry 'Hooky' Moulton selecting a float from his tackle box before taking part in a 1960s fishing match.

Fifteen-year-old David Holman landed this massive eel on 12 October 1963.

The Wyche Anglers fishing team celebrating their success in the all England fishing finals on 2 May 1964.

Mr G. Morris presenting the Hulme Cup at a Wyche Anglers Club evening on 17 November 1966.

Smiling trophy winners at the Wyche Anglers Club on 14 December 1967.

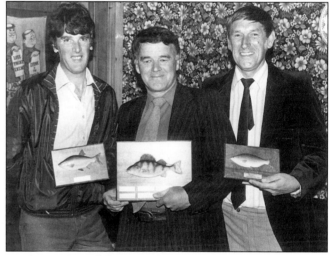

Wyche Anglers Club members at a presentation evening after successfully competing in an Angling Gala Week in 1982.

Prize winners of the White Horse Inn fishing match held at Henhull Bridge, Nantwich, on 13 November 1984, were, left to right: Mr B. Taylor, Mrs K. Barker, Mr Roy Stubbs, Mr T. Barker, Mr F. Walker, Mr A. Dale, Mr J. Ridgway and Mr Albert Barker. The first prize was won by the licensee, Mr J. Ridgway.

Darts

A 1950s darts team from the White Swan public house, Pillory Street.

Well-known sportsman, Mr Peter Moulton (right) receives a presentation from Mr A. Broomhall (captain of the Wonderboys Darts Team), to mark his wedding on 20 March 1955. The licensee of the Lamb Hotel is pictured in the centre of the group.

Nantwich Cricket Club's G.S. Ramchand (left) presenting the Vine Darts Trophy to champion Rol Ankers on 7 May 1955.

The Bowling Green Inn team who were division two champions of the Wednesday night darts league in 1955.

Frank Benoy (second from left) presenting the Friday Night League trophy to Arthur Broomhall on 21 May 1955.

Mr Price (centre) presents the trophy to the Shakespeare captain, S. Western, winners of the Nantwich charity darts competition, The Brooks Cup. On the right-hand side of the picture are the Cotton Arms captain, H. Spencer, J. Podmore and F. Stockton, 21 April 1956.

A Conservative Club darts presentation on 26 May 1956. Among those pictured are N. Sergeant, H. Clewlow, K. Elson, H. Hulse, J. Wainwright, K. Bickerton, E. Slack, C. Johnson and T. McGowan.

Mr Jim Harvey receiving The Benoy Trophy from Mr W. Hulme (centre), after winning the British Legion Darts Competition on 2 June 1956. Other competitors and officials look on.

The Farmers Arms darts team 20 October 1956.

The Shakespeare darts team on 22 December 1956.

The Union Vaults darts team pictured on 29 December 1956.

The Boot and Shoe darts team on 2 February 1957. Captain S. Speed is pictured second from the left, seated.

The Bowling Green Hotel darts team on 6 April 1957.

The British Legion Darts individual champion receiving his trophy on 5 July 1958.

Union Vaults, winners of the Friday Darts League on 9 May 1959. Showing Arthur Eaton (right centre), receiving the trophy from Bill Jones.

The Royal Oak darts team, Worleston, in the 1960s.

A darts presentation at the Railway Hotel on 9 April 1960.

The Bears Paw darts team on 23 April 1960.

The Cotton Arms darts team who won the Charity Darts Trophy on 28 May 1960.

Darts pairing Alan Smith (left) and Johnny Pimlott in the early 1960s.

The Vine, winners of the Greenall Whitley Champion Darts Trophy on 8 April 1961. John Driver, Greenall Whitley's area manager, is pictured centre, flanked by, Frank Edge (left) and Ernie Challinor.

Members of the Dysart 'A' Darts team on 22 April 1961. Back row, right to left: J. Rogerson, V. Mulliner, N. Simister, T. Matthews and R. Dutton. Front row: D. Edge, T. Laye (captain) and licensee, T. Moore.

Mr Arthur Broomhall (centre), presenting the winners cup to Farmers Arms captain, Jack Molyneux on 6 May 1961.

The Vine Inn team captain, Ernie Challinor, seated centre, surrounded by other Nantwich Darts League winners and officials in 1961.

Arthur Edwards (second left) receiving his trophy after winning the Nantwich British Legion Individual competition in 1962. Also pictured are left to right: Brian Tanzey, Cyril Welsh, Sydney Titley and chairman Colin Edwards.

The Vine darts team on 24 March 1962 with their captain, M. Dodd receiving the Chronicle Cup from Tom Lloyd (right).

Mrs T. Moore presenting the John Barnett Cup to the Dysart captain, J. Large watched by team members and officials on 28 April 1962.

The Shakespeare players who competed in the Nantwich Friday Night Darts League in 1963.

The Davenport Arms darts team who took part in the John Barnett Darts Competition in 1963.

The Nags Head darts team pictured on 18 February 1964.

Nantwich LV darts awards on 8 June 1963. Pictured are: Ernie Challinor, Jim Ridgeway, Jack Hughes, Frank Ruscoe and Tommy Lloyd.

One of the youngest teams in the Nantwich LV League in 1965 were this team from the Three Pigeons in Welsh Row.

The Vine Inn, Shavington, champions of the Nantwich Friday Night Darts League on 19 November 1965.

The Oddfellows darts team of 2 December 1965.

Nantwich Friday Night League darts team, the Lord Combermere pictured on 16 December 1965.

The Millfields darts team on 29 September 1966.

The Lord Combermere darts team on 6 October 1966.

The Lamb public house, Willaston, darts team on 20 October 1966.

The Boot and Shoe darts team 1966.

Wybunbury Red Lion 'B' team on 3 November 1966.

The BBB darts team which played at The Talbot pictured on 8 December 1966.

Winners of the Friday Night Darts League in 1967 were this team from the Star public house.

The BBB's team who played in the Nantwich Licenced Victuallers League in 1967.

The Royal Oak 'A' darts team on 20 April 1967.

Mrs J.O. Jones presenting the John Barnett Cup to Peter France, captain of the Tollemarche Arms, Alpraham, darts team on 27 April 1967. Also pictured are left to right: T. Oakes, J.O. Jones and William Lovett captain of the runner-up Starlings darts team.

The Bridge Inn darts team Audlem in 1967.

Nantwich Town chairman, Tom Holman, presenting the Combermere Arms captain, Horace Stevenson, with the trophy on 18 May 1967.

The Wednesday Darts League AGM on 21 September 1967. Among those pictured are Ken Ashley, Colin Harding, Eric Sutton, Bob Dykes, Ted Slack, Snug Betteley and Tommy Lloyd.

Brooks Charity darts finalists on 8 June 1967.

The Talbot, winner of the LV Darts League in 1968.

Mrs M. Brassington presenting the cups to Mr Jack Molyneux (right) captain of the Starlings darts team, and Brian Ashbrook, captain of the runners-up team, The Tollemarche Arms on 25 April 1968.

Chronicle reporter, Alan Jervis, presenting the Brooks Charity Darts Cup on 6 June 1968.

Winners of the Friday Night Darts League in 1968 were the Lord Combermere.

A Nantwich Wednesday night darts presentation evening for the Summer League winners in 1973.

Cricket

Herbie Sandlands receiving his award from Councillor Guy Harvey for scoring 100 not out and taking all 10 wickets for the Boot and Shoe team in the Nantwich Cricket Knock-out competition in 1952 at the Jackson Avenue football ground.

Nantwich British Legion team who were runners-up in the Nantwich Knock-out Cricket Final on 18 July 1953. Standing (left to right): L.A. Hoff (umpire), B. Bowton, D. Lloyd, W. Hodgkinson, F. Sherratt, H. Cooke, W. Dickens, L.A. Parker (social secretary). Seated: S. Hope, W. French, C. Edwards (captain), G. Owen, T. Davies. (On the floor) J. Williamson.

The North Western Gas Board cricket team on 5 September 1953.

Harry Cimelli getting signatures to a petition to try to save the Kingsley Fields Cricket Ground on 28 January 1956. Alas, his efforts were unsuccessful.

Eric Robinson (left), showing *Chronicle* reporter, Eddie Baskeyfield, the proposed new site of the Nantwich Cricket Club ground in Whitehouse Lane – its present home – on 18 August 1956.

Haighton's Factory cricket team, winners of the Nantwich Knock-out competition in 1953.

England Test star Len Hutton, pictured during a visit to the Nantwich Cricket Club in the 1950s. Also in the picture are, left to right: John Ikin, Joe Sproston, Ted Stevenson, Mal Wetton, Howard Platt, Tom Maybury and Herbert Bennett.

The Boot and Shoe who took part in the 1954 Nantwich Cricket Knock-out competition. Back row: T. Ormes (umpire), H. Sandlands, H. Oakes, F. Cliffe, J. Heath, and N. Oakes. Front row: F. Everall, H. Cowap, A. Stubbs (captain), J. Prince, L. Foster, and B. Tew.

The Nantwich 2nd XI cricket team on 18 May 1957. Back row (left to right): A. Astbury, E. Marsh, C. Metcalf, J. Cooper, J. Robinson and F. Everall. Front row: P. Swindells, D. Ridyard, B. Woodbridge, D. Morgan and J. Prince.

The United Dairies cricket team, winners of the Tattenhall Knock-out competition on 17 July 1957.

A Nantwich Grammar School Cricket team in 1957.

Young local cricketers on 23 July 1960 (left to right): Brian Griffiths, Robert Humphries and Michael Taylor.

Nantwich chairman, Mr Joe Blagg presenting the captain of The Assortments team with the Nantwich Knock-out cricket trophy after they won the final on 20 August 1960.

A Nantwich Cricket Club first XI in 1954.

The Nantwich Young Farmers cricket team which won the Cheshire Young Farmers club branches knock-out competition in 1961.

Banks and Braes cricket team with their trophies in 1961.

A Nantwich cricket team which took part in the Nantwich Knock-out competition in the early 1960s. Back row: Jack Bell, Bernard Pennell, Jim Tew, Albert Nicholls, John Broomhall, Fred Perry and Tommy Hope. Front row: not known, Alf Wheeler, not known, not known, Ronnie Reade and Billy Walsh.

Joe Sproston congratulating Harry Woodcock at a Nantwich Cricket Knock-out presentation evening on 13 April 1963. Looking on are Mr Williams, Albert Parker, Len Cooke, Les Hoff and Jack Wright.

Weston Wanderers cricket team on 25 May 1963.

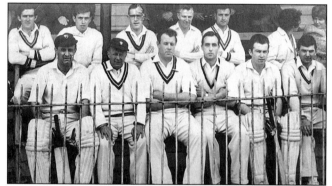

Nantwich Cricket Club team, early 1960s.

North Western Farmers Knock-out cricket team on 25 May 1963.

The Rifleman cricket team photographed on 1 June 1963.

The Post Office cricket team which took part in the Nantwich Cricket Knock-out competition on 29 June 1963.

A Nantwich Young Farmers team which played in the Nantwich Cricket Knock-out competition on 6 July 1963.

The Nantwich Odds and Ends Knock-out cricket team on 13 July 1963.

The Crewe Line CC who took part in the Nantwich Knock-out competition in 1963.

The Cheshire Senior Schools cricket team pictured on 15 August 1964.

Nantwich Marauders cricket team take the field on 5 September 1964.

Park Drive Cricket Club in the 1960s.

The North Western Farmers Accounts cricket team pictured on 26 June 1966.

Dr Walley presenting a cheque to the Audlem Cricket Club on 3 November 1966.

Audlem Cricket Club team pictured on 4 May 1967.

The Park Drivers team who beat a strong Wrenbury Young Farmers cricket team on 18 May 1967 in the Nantwich Knock-out Cup.

The Nantwich Knock-out cricket team, the Dakotas on 8 June 1967.

The Untouchables cricket team on 15 June 1967.

The White Lion Wanderers, Weston, cricket team on 6 July 1967.

The Assortments cricket team who played in the Nantwich Knock-out Cup on 6 July 1967.

The Gunners Cricket Club team, 13 July 1967.

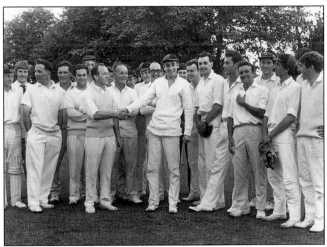

Nantwich and Acton Grammar School captain, Mr Brown, shaking hands with Old Grammar captain Peter Bebbington prior to a cricket match at the school on 27 July 1967.

A team which took part in the Nantwich Cricket Knock-out competition on 17 August 1967. Peter Swindells is holding the trophy.

The Burton Hotel cricket team, which took part in the Nantwich Knock-out competition on 31 August 1967.

Nantwich Young Farmers cricket team captain, David Latham, receiving the winners trophy on 7 September 1967.

Nantwich Cricket Club AGM in the late 1960s. Seated: Reg Windsor, Arthur Hassall, Albert Parker and Terry Parkinson.

Andrew Bee receives the cricket club trophy at the Audlem presentation evening on 1 February 1968.

Nantwich CC 1st XI skipper Ray Sherratt welcoming the 1975 professional, Gupti, as his new teammates look on.

Audlem Cricket Club squad, league winners in the 1978 season.

Members of the Nantwich Cricket Club with members of an Indian touring team before their match at Whitehouse Lane Ground in the early 1980s.

Nantwich CC's 1995 team with skipper Andy Newton, middle front.

Dominoes

The Oddfellows domino team in 1953, back row (left to right): E. Preece, F. Tomkinson, W. Palin, A. Tomkinson, J. Moore, J. Williamson (licensee). Front row: T. Mullinor, E. Mellor, J. Sherratt and J. Sharpes.

The Liberal Club domino team which played in division two in 1953. Back row (left to right): W.E. Jones (steward), W. Western, E. Wilkes, W. Collett, (club secretary), N. Prawl. Front row: F. Prince, R. Blackburn, J. Rheade, J. Hughes and G. Smith.

The White Horse team which played in division one of the Nantwich Domino League in 1953. Back row (left to right): J. Rowley, J. Ridgway, F. Walker, L. Davies, K. Bickerton. Front row: J. Bradbury, T. Dutton, M. McGowan (captain), G. Stanton and G. Perry.

The Three Pigeons domino team which competed in division two in 1953. Back row, left to right: J. Broadhurst, N. Fisher, H. Whittingham, F. Burrows, J. Podmore, W. Harvey, L. Clough, T. Bowton. Front row: T. Cartwright, G. Welsh, G. Morgan, J. Cooke and J. Lang.

The Black Lion domino team on 31 October 1953. Back row, left to right: E. Larwards, J. Basford, J. Franklyn, J. Belfield, H. Johnson. Front row: F.B. Darlington, G. Slack, C. Williamson and K. Carroll.

The Old Vaults domino team on 12 December 1953. Back row (left to right): D. Ralphs, T. Whittles, W. Greenwood, S. Metcalfe, R. Reade. Front row: G. Davies, L. Gott, F. Astles (manager), W. Weaver and M. Beresford.

This division one domino team pictured on 2 January 1954 are the Boot and Shoe. Back row (left to right): A. Hodgkinson, W. Cooke (licensee), L. Lester, J. Bullimor, T. Faukner, K. Bourne and R. Humphreys. Front row: S. Mason, H. Chesters, A. Cartwright, G.W. Owen, K. Brookes and H. Evans.

Division two leaders on 22 February 1954 were this Red Lion domino team. Left to right standing: J. Dobson, T. Birch, S. Warner, W. Jones. Seated: H. Kent, G. Jackson, F. Chesters (captain), W. Foxley and L. Jones.

The Royal Oak domino team of 13 March 1954.

The Cheshire Cheese domino team which played in division two in 1954. Back row (left to right): A. Farrington, H. Simpson, W. Wright, G. Smith, J. Moss, G. Jackson. Seated: R. Ellearton (captain), S. Ankers and N. Morris.

The Game Cock team playing in the Nantwich Domino League division two in 1954. Standing (left to right): E. Betteley, E. Metcalf, F. Ruscoe, J. Reade, H. Bibby, G. Nevitt. Seated: B. Holmes, J. Cookson, J. Jackson, H. Sharratt, D. Edmonds.

Nantwich domino team, division one in 1954 were The Rifleman. Back row (left to right): S. Johnson (secretary), H. Goodwin, A. Hughes (captain), G. Condrey senior, H. Burgess junior, A. Willett. Front row: W. Dimelow, R. Wakefield, W. Alard, T. Parrott.

This Union Vaults domino team played in division one in the 1954 season. Pictured are, left to right: D. Belfield, W. Maclean, A. Eaton (centre), E. Farrington, L. Wainwright, F. Moss. Front row: C. Jones, W. Johnson, H. Boden (licensee) and F. Jones.

The Crosville team which played in division one of their domino league in 1954. Back row, left to right: R. Heath, J. Davies, M. McClymont, G. Bailey. Front row: B. Rogers, J. Sergeant, R. Dutton and H. Buclley.

The Bowling Green domino team who played in division two in 1954. Back row (left to right): M. Chapman, T. Peake, F.W. Peake (licensee), A. Sewell, A. Bossons. Front row: E. Betteley, F. FLeet, R. Jackson (captain), H. Jones and W. Mason.

This Red Cow domino team of 1954 included three brothers and an uncle. Seated, left to right: J. Cornes, W. Ormes, G. Hayes, F. Sherratt. Standing: P.Johnson, D. Rowe, R. Sherratt, H. Sherratt and J. Sherratt (uncle).

The Union Vaults domino team on 2 April 1955.

Mr Guy Harvey who made the presentations on 30 April 1955 is pictured with the winning team captains at the Nantwich Domino League's annual prize distribution at the Lamb Hotel, Willaston. Left to right: M. McGowan (White Horse), K. Kent (Red Lion), A.E. Wetton (The Lamb, Willaston), Mr Harvey, W. Johnson (Union Vaults), J. Hughes (The Royal Oak) and L. Spears (The Leopard).

The all smiling Oddfellows domino team who played in division two in the 1956 season.

The Leopard public house domino team on 9 February 1957. Licensee and former boxer, Jackie Potts is seated second left on the front row.

The Old Veterans domino team which played in the Nantwich League in 1958 and had a combined age of 721 years!

The Nantwich Liberal Club domino team on 7 February 1959.

The Nantwich Domino League presentations on 2 May 1959.

Domino prize winners and officials at a presentation evening on 6 May 1961. Among those pictured are: Jim Hodgkinson, Ken Danskin, Ernie Betteley, Bill Ormes, Jack Wareham, Ronnie Ward, Jack Podmore, Jack Molyneux and Harry Jones.

A Wickstead Arms domino team of 7 April 1962.

A smiling Laurie Gilfedder (centre) presents Dominoes League players with their trophy on 5 May 1962.

The Wickstead Arms domino team who defeated the Three Pigeons 'B' team on 30 March 1963.

The Oddfellow's championship winning domino team of 1963.

Members of the Game Cock and Red Cow domino teams ham it up for the camera before competing in the opening game of the new season on 26 September 1964.

The Black Lion, champions of the Nantwich Domino League in 1964.

The Conservative Club 'B' domino team on 21 October 1965.

The Wilbraham Arms when they were promoted to the first division of the Nantwich Domino League on 2 December 1965.

Domino League secretary, Bill Ormes, flanked by officials, gets to work at the 1966 annual general meeting.

The Royal Oak domino team had one of their most successful seasons in 1967.

Nantwich domino league winners 20 June 1968.

The Wyche Anglers domino team of 1969.

Other Sport

Nantwich Amateur Boxing Club members pictured during a training evening on 26 September 1959.

Perhaps one of the most popular local boxers was the late Jackie Potts who was landlord of the Leopard Hotel in London Road, Nantwich, for many years.

Paddy Porter (centre) winner of the Nantwich ABC Chatwin Trophy in 1963.

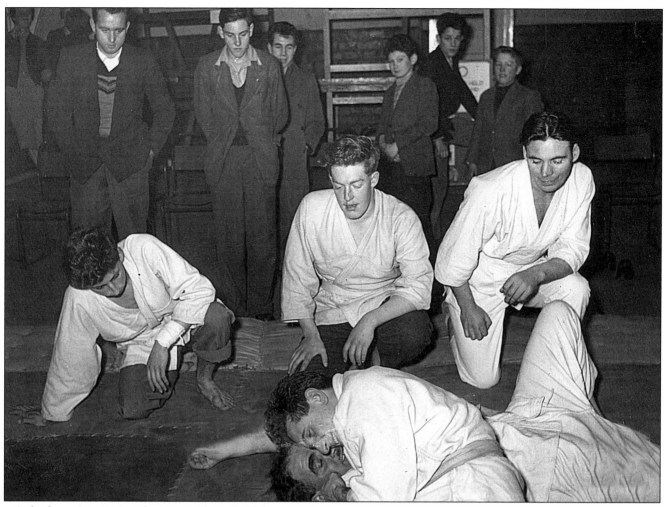

A judo demonstration at the Nantwich Boy's Club on 19 January 1957.

Nantwich Boys' Club judo team who competed in on 3 June 1961.

The Cheshire Schools hockey team on 22 December 1966.

Nantwich and Acton Grammar School hockey team on 30 May 1958.

Proprietor Harry Sandland passing on tips to the local youths at Nantwich Billiard Hall on 5 October 1963.

Snooker and billiards awards night at the Nantwich Liberal Club on 28 September 1963.

Nantwich Young Farmers competing in the annual sports day at the Reaseheath Agricultural College in May 1963. The start of the mens 100 yds race.

The start of the ladies 100 yard race.

Some of the many winners at the Nantwich Motor Club dinner dance and awards evening on 13 February 1959.

A group of major award winners at the Nantwich Motor Club dinner dance on 6 February 1965.

Hospital Street Methodist Church badminton team in the 1950s. Back row: J. Sproston, C. Bull, E.C. Sutton, and L. Williamson. Front row: Mrs C. Young, Miss D. Thomas, Mrs R. Mason and Mrs F. Furber.

The Nantwich Old Grammarians badminton team, second division champions of the Crewe and District Badminton League in the 1952-53 season. Left to right (back row): D. Thompson, A.L. Howarth, P. Moulton, P. Edwards and H. Hull. Front row: Miss S. Patrick, Mrs A.L. Hawarth, Miss B.H. Hinde, Mrs H. Cowap and Miss H. Heath.

The Hospital Street 'B' team who won the Crewe and District Badminton Division Two Mixed League on 4 April 1964.

Players who took part in a 1980s Crewe and District Badminton League tournament in the 1980s.

Pretty Ella Miles who played badminton for England in 1990.

Trophy winners and officials at the 1959 Nantwich tennis tournament on 16 May 1959.

Competitors and officials at the Nantwich Junior tennis tournament on 17 August 1967.

Nantwich Young Farmers Club annual general meeting showing prize winners and officials on 12 December 1964.

Young Farmers Club chairman, Mr Richard Latham (centre) with trophy winners at the 1962 YFC tennis finals.

Mr Mellor presenting the supreme award to Mr Colin Chesters (extreme right) at the Nantwich Premier Flying Club awards night on 2 December 1965.

Members of the Nantwich Amateur Swimming Club line up for a photograph in 1964.

Nantwich schoolboy, Paul Tew, pictured on his arrival home after swimming the English Channel in 1976.

Nantwich Club chairman, Mr E.J. Hinde pictured with young swimmers at the Nantwich Swimming Baths in the 1960s.

Members of the Beeston Gun club pictured at a shoot on 17 May 1958.

Lady Helen Delves Broughton receiving expert instruction from Beeston Gun Club members on 9 September 1961.

Mr Vernon Cooper (left), pictured with family members before leaving to take part in the Tulpen Rallye on 1 May 1954.

Nantwich Boys Club members on 25 May 1968.

Motorcycle scrambler, Alan Clough at a Hatherton
meeting on 30 September 1961.

A Hatherton scramble on 17 August 1967.

A Crewe to Nantwich charity fun run in the 1990s.